SECRETS OF MY PAIN

SECRETS OF MY PAIN

JAMEKA MCCULLOUGH

Jameka McCullough

To anyone that is dealing with pain from everyday struggles to relationships, the words in this book is for you. Remember to take it one day at a time!

Jameka

Copyright © 2020 by Jameka McCullough

All rights reserved. No part of this book may be reproduced in any manner whatsoever without written permission except in the case of brief quotations embodied in critical articles and reviews.

First Printing, 2020

I

My Regret

Broke like a withered flower

Heart empty happiness faded away

My thoughts of you still haunt me from my mistake

I wonder how you would have been now

What your eye color would have been

Would your hair be curly like mine?

Would you be protective over me and your brother?

The thoughts of you makes me cry

I see your beautiful face in my dreams

I feel so empty without you here

Regret hits me like the snow hits the mountain

Until my last breath your face will stay with me

The love will never fade

My sorrow will shines like a nonstop thunderstorm

Empty

As the sunset settles down, the lonely state sits in

Trapped in the inner thoughts that are harm the outer appearance

There is no other way to turn or go

Hiding in the darkness has taken over

Shutting down seems to be the only to cope with everything

Wanting and needing someone to hear me

But my pride just will not let me be free of these inner thoughts and actions

It is getting darker and as the sunsets so does my peace and the pain eats up my mind

Power

The power to love

The power to feel

The power to fight

The power to overcome

The power to encourage

The strength to heal

The strength to empower

The strength to be true to yourself

The strength to have faith

This is a true definition of a powerful black woman

My Ending

Sitting in an empty room crying out for help

The voices are taking over

Pressuring me to finish what was started

I am fighting to not let it all go but the other side seems easier

I lay down on the floor with a blade in hand

I press it so hard against my wrist until it bleeds

I close my eyes hoping to leave peacefully

My letter has been written, my plans are coming together

I take one last deep breath and soon it all ends

Now I am at peace

Now I am at home

Now I can be free from the pain and the thoughts

Now I have broken the life I gave

Now he has no one

Now he is all alone

My selfishness has taken over and left my love stranded

It is too late to come back

Now the cycle of pain continues....

Broken Flower

The broken flower that was once blooming

Has fell deep through the roots

The water that once help the beautiful flower grow

Has gone away and is now watering another flower

The brokenness of the flower is struggling to feel life again

Through the roughest times of the seasons the flower finds its way

Eventually the flower is finally back to a place where it is ready to be watered again

A Daughter's Cry

She is sitting in a dark room staring at out the window

She is in deep thought about the words that was said to her

She is crying and her heart is broken from the pain inside

She is slowly drifting away from life as she stares out into the world

What has caused this pain she is enduring?

In her thoughts all you can see is her mother talking to her

The words coming out are hurtful and dismissive

Her mother does not understand how much she is killing her

All she wants is just a hug or love that is missing

She wants the trust and assurance that everything will be ok

All she is getting is judgement and dismissive feelings and emotions

When will this pain go away?

When will she finally get the love she is searching for?

As she continues to stare out the window this pain grows stronger

As her mind dissolved away

She is finally at her end

As she closes her eyes her world has ended.

Questions

What do I do in this situation?

I feel like I keep putting myself into these situations

I need to let go

Even though it will be hard to do

All I am doing is hurting myself in the end

Ask them these few questions

If they cannot answer them then you have your answers

1. If I needed you right now would you answer the phone?
2. If something were to happen to me would you be there for me?
3. If I died today would you even miss me or shed a tear?

Purpose of Life

Strength courage and wisdom are the key to life

These three powerful words can get you through

Even in the toughest battles and times in your life

Strength to fight your daily struggles

Courage to believe you will make it through

Wisdom to know there is more to life than pain

Strength to press on

Courage to keep your head up

Wisdom to know living every day to its fullest

Strength to take that next step

Courage to keep pushing

Wisdom to believe in yourself

Distant Memory

If I died tomorrow would you miss me

If I were to get hurt would you be there

If I needed you the most would you stand by me

Would you even cry if you never heard my voice again?

Would you even think about me if you didn't see me again?

Would you ever wonder where I went if o disappeared?

Would you even think or feel anything?

Would you ever be there for me anymore?

As time goes by, we are drifting away

As time goes by you don't even notice

As time goes by, I am slowly disappearing from you

As time passes you don't even care

As time passes by, our conversation is less important

As time passes by, we will eventually become strangers

As time passes by, I will only be a distant memory

Inner Thoughts

My mind is filled like the clouds in the sky

It is filled with all kinds of wonders and worries

I wonder if I kissed your lips will you still feel anything

I wonder if I just hugged you, the way I use to

Would you still think of me?

I wonder if I touched you, the way I use to

Would you feel anything

I wonder if I calm down and let go

Would you come back to me

I worry about if you would push me away

If I tried to kiss your lips to see

If the love is still there

I worry about if I hug you

Would it give us the same feeling as before?

I worry about if I touched you

Would you let me

I worry about if I don't let you breathe

Would you ever come back to me?

My cloudy thoughts keep me up at night

Just like a thunderstorm in the night

I wonder so much

I fear so much

I worry so much

I still feel so much

One day these cloudy thoughts will soon fade away

Feelings

You will never understand the way I feel about you

My anger is still hurt

My love is still strong

My pain is still there

Saying you care does not mean anything

Your actions tell me different

I wish things were different

Sorry my timing was never right for you

Guess I am still not going to ever be good enough

Don't worry about my struggle

I am used to dealing with it alone

I will be ok

You will be ok without me in your life

Love who you want to love

Don't take it for granted

I will be ok

No Love

It is late and I cannot sleep

All I can think about is you loving someone else

You want to be with this person

You are happy with this person

And here I am lonely again

Broken again

I cannot but the blame on you

It is my fault my problem

I know it doesn't matter to what I say anymore

If love is like this, I don't want it anymore

I rather be alone then feeling this way

I already feel so worthless and not good enough

I am starting to see that it is true

Everything I touch goes bad

What's the point in being here?

Don't tell me life is great

I have lost life

It may take days weeks or even months to get over you

Even through the hurt for some reason I still want to fight for you

I don't think I have anything else to give

You will never understand my love

I guess I have to deal with that

I am sorry I wasn't the one for and sorry I even came in your life all I did was mess things up for you instead of making it better

Openness

My heart is like a piece of ice that melted when I first saw you

My cold heartedness was warmed by your beautiful smile and gentle eyes

My soul found love again

My mind was at ease

My love grows stronger

My happiness grew so deep within

My love for you will never change

Hopefully, I taught you something great

Remember the great times of the love I gave

Just like the beautiful flower that blossom into something great

Peace will be at ease deep inside

As my peace will end

No Escape

Trapped in my own mind

Don't know how to make it stop

People thinking you're just mean

In reality you're fighting yourself daily

No outlet no release

What do you do?

The struggle of your thoughts taking over

The pain you feel everyday

The fear of the end

The loneliness you feel

The constant back and forth

The anger you feel inside

The hate you wish you don't have

The love you desire

Understanding you hope for

What do you do?

How do you figure it out?

The sleepless nights

The tears you shed

The words you tell people

The cry for help

Even when nobody hears you

Nobody really understands

Why should they?

Even when you pray constantly

What's left to do?

Give up or keep fighting

The struggles of everyday life

The struggle of yourself

Loss of words

Nothing left to give

....

Decisions

My faith is being tested so bad...

I just want to give up...

I am at a lost...

I am confused stressed out

I am losing it...

I am about to snap

Should I end it all

Or should I keep holding on

I know others may have it worse than me

But I am still human

My emotions are fucked up

I am starting my old habits again

Don't know what to do anymore

Crazy World

This world is crazy

What have we become in this world?

Different races hating each other more and more

All the killings and fighting are progressing

this world we once had is shattered

Babies and kids dying everyday

Our young generation is lost

No education no morals

No self-love

No guidance

No remorse

See I pray for each and every person I see

I don't know what kind of struggle they battle

See my heart is too kind

My mind is too proud

I love seeing people succeed

I love seeing people prevail

I may not have money

I may not be the best person I can be

But I know my heart will always be kind

No matter the struggle we should all still have the love for one another

Man, I know this world is crazy

I know there is always going to be someone hating me

Whether it is because the color of my skin

Whether it is my religion

Whether it is my political views

Whether if it is my gender

Hell, maybe it is my sexuality

But that will never stop me from trying to make in this world

See I am going to succeed

I am going to prevail

I am going to progress

I am still going to pray

I am still going to love those who hate me

I am still going to believe there is life

See I am still going to live day by day

Until God calls me home

I am worth something

You are worth something

We as a whole are worth more than anything in this world

So be who you are

Love everyone

Live life to the fullest

Humble yourself each and every day

Peaceful Angel

Gentle humble angel you finally got your wings

A beautiful soul is finally at peace

Your humbleness and kind heart touch many people

Your gentle smile warmed up our heart

Your sweetheart enlightened our souls

We remember you as the happy person you were

Our strong fighting solider that fought to the end

Strain Thoughts

My mind is wondering

It's going a million miles per hour

Not knowing is stressful

I am afraid of what is to come

The feeling of losing something or someone

Special is hurtful

I do not think my heart can take any more hurt

When I finally let my guard down

It seems like that is when I get hurt the most

I hate to think like that

Maybe I am looking into the situation wrong

It is just the feeling I am getting and the silence

Is killing me

The Unknown

My mind is going 500mph and I do not know how to stop it...

I am trying to escape but nobody is around

I am crying for help, but nobody is listening

I am lost and need something, so I pick up a bottle to ease my pain it is not working, and tears do not matter I am alone and afraid my past is back

I am struggling to breathe just need someone there as I lay down and take my last breath into the night

I ask myself what's life

I am at a dark spot and I am all alone

All my feelings are numb, and I do not know how to escape

I just want to be free and not let my problems get the best of me

I just want someone to understand

I do not mean any harm

I just do not know how to be free of myself...

Maybe this will be my last

Maybe I should not be here

What is the purpose I feel like every time I am ok something else fails?

I am tired and do not know what to do anymore......

Restless Mind

What do you do when you have no one to turn to?

Right now, I feel broken inside and do not know why...

My attitude is my cry out for help

When I am silent, I am back in a dark place that I fight everyday

To be honest I do not know why I am here on this earth...

I do not know my purpose in life and a lot of things I want to say

I am afraid to open up

I do not want anyone to throw it back in my face...

My soul is lost, and I try to smile to keep from crying, but my mind will not let my heart stop aching...

I hide what I am really feeling because I already see the outcome...

-thoughts of a restless person

Wishful Thinking

My heart is not easily influenced like it used to be when it got its chance to finally love someone.

The more the heartbreak the more cold-hearted it became.

She is very hard to break through but if you're a strong enough man to handle the good the bad the ugly then trust the ice will melt and you will have someone that will love harder than you can ever imagine. It is going to take time to find your way just know it is not going to be easy to do but it can be done...

One can think oh I may lose in the end to someone else yes that could be true

Thinking that way you already lost her because in her eyes you are already defeated without trying...

Pray about it

Trust she is doing the same about you whether you know it or not......

Pieces of Life

My soul is so lost

I can't comprehend what is going on

My world is turned upside down

My heroes are broken

My ancestors are not pleased

My fight is beginning to fade-away

My people are dying

I'm fearing for our children

I can't see my future anymore

I can only pray for today

My questions are flowing constantly

My answers are not being heard

My life is in danger

Just because of my skin color

My purpose is still unclear

What more can my people endure

Are we too hardheaded

Are we too stubborn

Are we to prideful

Why do we hate each other

But then blame other kinds for what we do to each other daily

This is our punishment

This is our test

This is the time to grow

This is the time to build with each other

Once we can conquer our hatred for each other

Once we come together

We as feared people will be stronger than ever

We can overcome anything

We will be powerful

We will be everything our ancestors fought and died for

Our prayers will finally be answered

Lightning Source UK Ltd.
Milton Keynes UK
UKHW020635011122
411449UK00017B/640